The Giving Church

Living by the Lighthouse Principles

KIRK NOWERY

Published by Spire Resources, Inc.
PO Box 180, Camarillo, CA 93011
1-800-992-3060

Portions of this book have been adapted from *The 33 Laws of Stewardship*, published by Spire Resources.

Scripture quotations are taken from the HOLY BIBLE: NEW INTERNA-TIONAL VERSION®. Copyright © 1973, 1978, 1984 by International Bible Society. Used by permission of Zondervan Publishing House.

Cover and text design by Bill Thielker

Printed in the United States of America

ISBN 0-9715828-5-8

CONTENTS

CONTENTS

PREFACE

Metaphorically, the church is many things—a body, a family, a household, a kingdom, a priesthood, a flock. These and other scriptural pictures deepen our understanding of what the church is and how it functions. And to these descriptive images I would add one more: a lighthouse. Admittedly, I don't have a Bible verse to attach to this concept, but I often think of the church with this picture in mind.

I have been at sea on many occasions when the reassuring presence of a lighthouse made the difference between safety and calamity. A church, like a lighthouse, is a powerful source of illumination, constantly giving warning, direction, confidence, help and encouragement. When I consider all that a lighthouse represents and all that it does, to me it depicts ideally the essence of this book, *The Giving Church*.

This is a book about principles—what I have termed lighthouse principles. These are irrefutable truths with an impact that is deep and lasting, and often life-changing. And each one is linked directly to the spiritual priority of giving. These are not man-made opinions but God-given precepts with the capacity to transform our thinking and crystallize our priorities.

The Giving Church is a practical book, not a theological treatise. It combines biblical examples, illustrations and memorable thoughts to zero in on specific principles. Each chapter concludes with a section entitled Practicing the Principles, which provide real-life applications.

Like other books I have written in this genre, *The Giving Church* takes a whole-life view of stewardship. After all, stewardship isn't just about money. It touches virtually every aspect of life and everything God puts into our hands. I hope that you will be blessed by the devotional emphasis in these chapters because *The Giving Church* is really about Christ-centered living. May it benefit you as a steward and enrich your life with wisdom.

1

CAN YOU KEEP A SECRET?

*Godly giving is a private demonstration,
not a public display.*

Abraham had to wait a quarter of a century—25 long years—before the promised son was born. By then he was 100 years old; his wife, Sarah, was 90. Yet God superceded the laws of nature to allow the birth of a child to an elderly, barren couple. They named their son Isaac, meaning "laughter," because he brought unspeakable joy to them.

After Isaac had grown into young manhood, God commanded Abraham to give an extraordinary offering: "Take your son, your only son, Isaac, whom you love, and go to the region of Moriah. Sacrifice him there as a burnt offering on one of the mountains I will tell you about."[1]

Obediently, Abraham took his boy on that long, agonizing trip to the bleak slopes of Mt. Moriah. Though he did not comprehend God's purpose, Abraham's faith was not shaken. He complied with the instructions, placing his dear son on the altar and raising a knife to plunge into the young man's chest. At the very moment he lifted the knife to slay his son, God stopped him. The Lord commanded Abraham to sacrifice instead a ram that was caught in a nearby bush.

We wonder: Would he have gone through with it? Would the old man have actually offered his own beloved son? The Bible gives us the answer: "Abraham reasoned that God could raise the dead, and figuratively speaking, he did receive Isaac back from death."[2] Yes, he would have done it, because he was already expecting God to raise his son from the dead!

No one was anywhere nearby when Abraham and Isaac were on that mountain. The offering to be given that day was a private offering, seen only by God. There in that remarkable situation so many centuries ago, a precept of stewardship was revealed: the Principle of Anonymous Giving.

There in that remarkable situation so many centuries ago, a precept of stewardship was revealed: the Principle of Anonymous Giving.

It's the same principle we discover in the words of Jesus: "Be careful not to do your acts of righteousness before men, to be seen by them. If you do, you will have no reward from your Father in heaven. So when you give...do not announce it with trumpets, as the hypocrites do in the synagogues and on the streets, to be honored by men. I tell you the truth, they have received their reward in full... Do not let your left hand know what your right hand is doing, so that your giving may be in secret. Then your Father, who sees what is done in secret, will reward you."[3]

With rare exceptions, giving is to be a private demonstration of obedience, not a public display of magnanimity.

With rare exceptions, giving is to be a private demonstration of obedience, not a public display of magnanimity. God is pleased when a gift is given with regard only for His purposes and His glory, completely devoid of any attention being drawn to the giver. To draw attention to oneself when giving is to express an attitude of ownership rather than stewardship. If you think that what you are giving is something you own instead of something that has been entrusted to you, you have eliminated God from the equation. The wise steward never forgets that everything belongs to God and every gift is made possible by Him alone.

PRACTICING THE PRINCIPLES

Don't draw attention to yourself; direct attention to the Lord. The Principle of Anonymous Giving reminds us that righteous giving is God-centered, not man-centered. To give in order to impress others with how spiritual we are actually denies our spirituality, and it is an affront to God. The believer's concern should never be with what people think but with what God thinks. If we live in a way that honors Him and gives Him glory, we don't have to worry about what people think. The one takes care of the other.

Don't measure yourself against other Christians. The standard we are to measure by is the character of Christ, not the character of other Christians. Paul had to address this problem in writing to the Corinthians: "We do not dare to classify or compare ourselves with some who commend themselves. When they measure themselves by themselves and compare themselves with themselves, they are not wise."[4] Peer pressure must not prompt one to give. The prompting of the Holy Spirit is to be our guide.

Don't forget the faith factor. The heart of Spirit-directed giving is faith. At the core of Abraham's willingness to give his own son was unbounded faith in the One who gave that son in the first place. As the Bible says, "Faith is being sure of what we hope for and certain of what we do not see."[5] In order to tap the endless resources of God, the believer must exercise faith by acting in obedience to God's Word. Paul explained to the Romans: "Faith comes by hearing, and hearing by the Word of God."[6] When one is prompted to give either by the Word of God or by the leadership of the Holy Spirit, obedience to that prompting is an expression of true spirituality.

Scripture References:
[1] Genesis 22:2
[2] Hebrews 11:19
[3] Matthew 6:1-4
[4] 2 Corinthians 10:12
[5] Hebrews 11:1
[6] Romans 10:17

2

—GIVING CONSISTENTLY—
ARE YOU CONSISTENTLY CONSISTENT?

Consistent giving empowers consistent ministry.

The impoverished Christians at Jerusalem were in dire straits. We don't know precisely why they were suffering so severely, but their situation was compellingly bad—so bad that the Apostle Paul instructed the believers in other places to take up a special offering for them. Paul reasoned that "if the Gentiles have shared in the Jews' spiritual blessings, they owe it to the Jews to share with them their material blessings."[1] But it was important that the offering be given in the right spirit and in the right way. They were to set aside an amount of money the first day of every week, in proportion to the Lord's blessing upon them during the week.

"Now about the collection for God's people: Do what I told the Galatian churches to do. On the first day of every week, each one of you should set aside a sum of money in keeping with his income, saving it up, so that when I come no collections will have to be made. Then, when I arrive, I will give letters of introduction to the men you approve and send them with your gift to Jerusalem."[2]

In the King James Version, a key phrase in this passage reads, "as the Lord had prospered..." The word "prospered" has a wonderful meaning in the original Greek language of the New Testament. Literally, it means "blessing in the good way." That "good way" might be a good way in business; it might be a good way in relationships; it might be a good way in deeper fellowship with God. And, while the essential idea is to give of our material wealth as God enables us to obtain it, there is also a prosperity of the soul that He gives. It is inadequate to measure our prosperity only in dollars and cents when He gives us so much in divine love, grace and mercy. We would be wise to think in terms of giving to God according to the full measure of His blessing. Imagine, for example, that each time He unfolded a new truth to you or answered a prayer or delivered you from danger, you would honor His gifts with an appropriate response. Imagine how much richer your life would be. In this larger context, financial gifts seem the very least we can do in obedience to the Lord and appreciation for His goodness.

It is inadequate to measure our prosperity only in dollars and cents when He gives us so much in divine love, grace and mercy.

The Principle of Consistent Giving, the spiritual law that is at the core of Paul's instruction in these verses, teaches us that *consistent giving empowers consistent ministry.* There isn't a legalistic demand that we

The ongoing operation of a church's ministry requires the ongoing support of faithful believers.

give a specified sum of money every week to the Lord's work, but that we give regularly and consistently. God's desire is that things be done decently and in order, not in chaos or uncertainty. When there is a need, His plan is that His people give responsively to meet it. The ongoing operation of a church's ministry, for example, requires the ongoing support of faithful believers. A majority of Christian leaders (myself included) believe that the foundation of God's plan for giving is the tithe—ten percent of one's income. Since ancient times, the tithe has been a standard (perhaps a minimum standard) for what one gives gratefully to God. In the first tithe described in the Bible, Abraham gave Melchizedek the high priest a tenth of everything he had. It was an expression of gratitude to God for victory and to God's priest for the sanctuary he had provided.[3]

PRACTICING THE PRINCIPLES

Consistent contributions to the Lord's work are acts of worship, expressions of devotion to Him. It is important that we give on a consistent, continuing basis because it demonstrates that we recognize the Lordship of Christ. The spirit in which we give is also important:

Give with consistent gratitude. Everything in our hands has come from His hand, and we are but channels through which God's work is carried out. When we live in primary consideration of Him, gratitude minimizes our tendencies to squander our resources on self-gratification.

Give with consistent sacrifice. David said, "I will not sacrifice to the Lord my God burnt offerings that cost me nothing"[4] Sacrifice always involves cost, but it has less to do with how much one gives than how much one gives up. In the measure of sacrifice, we must ask, What does this truly cost me? When we pay a sacrificial price in giving, we accentuate the sacred over the secular.

Give with consistent praise. The distinction between gratitude and praise is this: gratitude is appreciation for what God has done, praise is appreciation for who God is. King David knew the distinction: "Now our God, we give you thanks and praise your glorious name."[5] As you worship the Lord daily in times of meditation and prayer, remember that He is your provider and commit yourself consistently to being a good steward of His provision.

Scripture References:
[1] Romans 15:27
[2] 1 Corinthians 16:1-3
[3] Genesis 14:20
[4] 2 Samuel 24:24
[5] 1 Chronicles 29:13

3

WHAT ARE YOUR EXPECTATIONS?

Sow sparingly and you reap sparingly; sow bountifully and you reap bountifully.

In civil law, changes occur constantly as legislators— our "lawmakers"—debate and devise and decide the standards that govern our lives. Laws come and go as society evolves.

In criminal law, changes occur with less frequency but they do happen. For example, capital punishment was for many years allowed by the law, then for years it wasn't, then again it was. Such shifts are common in a complex, democratic system.

Many of God's spiritual laws have a counterpart in the physical world. None is more evident than the law of sowing and reaping.

In spiritual law, however, changes do not occur at all, for there is but one Lawmaker and He never changes. He is "the same yesterday, today and forever"[1] and His standards are fixed and permanent. Many of God's spiritual laws have a counterpart in the physical world, and none is more evident than the law of sowing and reaping. According to this law, whatever is sown always determines what is reaped. If you sow corn, you'll reap corn, not wheat or beans or rice. It is impossible to reap something different from what one has sown. The same truth applies in the spiritual dimension. The Scripture teaches: "Do not be deceived: God cannot be mocked. A man reaps what he sows. The one who sows to please his sinful nature, from that nature will reap destruction; the one who sows to please the Spirit, from the Spirit will reap eternal life. Let us not become weary in doing good, for at the proper time we will reap a harvest if we do not give up."[2]

There is an important corollary to the law of sowing and reaping, an essential principle of stewardship which we will call the Principle of Expectant Giving. Paul expressed it this way: "Remember this: Whoever sows sparingly will also reap sparingly, and whoever sows generously will also reap generously."[3] We find this same truth in the ancient Proverbs of King Solomon, many centuries before the time of Christ. He wrote, "A generous man will prosper; he who refreshes others will himself be refreshed."[4]

The promise of harvest is unalterable; it is totally in God's control. However, the decision as to what one sows is an individual decision. God doesn't force us to plant against our will; it's up to us to plant good seed and cultivate good crops in the soil of life. God's desire, clearly, is that we intentionally choose to plant and cultivate what is good, and to not give up in our well-doing. In daily stewardship this means consciously choosing to be generous, giving of ourselves and our resources without regard for the cost. If we do this, we can know what to expect. The unwearied doing of good produces an unfailing harvest of good.

The effective steward is a fruitful steward, one whose life is filled with the fruits of righteousness. This bounty is described in many ways throughout the Bible. Paul called it "the fruit of the Spirit," which he defined as nine virtues: "love, joy, peace, patience, kindness, goodness, faithfulness, gentleness and self-control."[5] The power that produces this fruit is spiritual power, the power of Christ dwelling in us. As Jesus said of Himself, "I am the vine; you are the branches. If a man remains in me and I in him, he will bear much fruit; apart from me you can do nothing. If anyone does not remain in me, he is like a branch that is thrown away and withers; such branches are picked up, thrown into the fire and burned. If you remain in me and my words remain in you, ask whatever you wish, and it will be given you. This is to my Father's glory, that you bear much fruit, showing yourselves to be my disciples."[6]

To "remain" or "abide" in Christ is to live in obedience to His commands. As He said, "If you obey my commands, you will remain in my love, just as I have obeyed my Father's commands and remain in his love."[7] The Christian who does not abide

The effective steward is a fruitful steward... and the power that produces this fruit is spiritual power, the power of Christ dwelling in us.

in Christ does not please God, and his works will be burned at the judgment seat of Christ. This does not refer to losing one's salvation; it has only to do with the fruit of one's life. The day of Christ's judgment will bring to light the reality of that harvest. "It will be revealed with fire, and the fire will test the quality of each man's work. If what he has built survives, he will receive his reward. If it is burned up, he will suffer loss; he himself will be saved, but only as one escaping the flames."[8]

PRACTICING THE PRINCIPLES

The Principle of Expectant Giving, like the law of sowing and reaping, is a truth that can clarify our thoughts and purify our motives. Remembering that we reap spiritually exactly what we have sown spiritually helps us to keep life in perspective and impels us to plant good seed at every opportunity. Remember these priorities:

Sow generously not sparingly. God gives us a supply of "seed" to be planted for His purposes. Whatever He supplies to you, sow it generously and wisely. Don't waste your time or resources sowing seeds of unrighteousness because all you'll get is a crop of weeds. Sow with an abundant intensity and you'll reap abundantly. That is a reasonable expectation.

Never give up in doing good. Sometimes Christians are mocked as "do-gooders." If it happens to you, let them mock, because you will ultimately be the winner; those who do good will reap a great harvest. Keep up the good work! Tenacity in well-doing is a sterling quality of stewardship.

Be patient. The spiritual harvest will come. It is a well-defined, well-ordered process that is in God's hands, not our own. Just as a physical crop comes in its own time and on its own terms, the spiritual crop cannot be rushed. We till the ground, we sow the seed, we cultivate the plants, but God gives the increase for He and He alone is Lord of the Harvest.

Scripture References:
1 Hebrews 13:8
2 Galatians 6:7-9
3 2 Corinthians 9:6
4 Proverbs 11:25
5 Galatians 5:22-23
6 John 15:5-8
7 John 15:10
8 1 Corinthians 3:13-15

4

—GIVING FAITHFULLY—
CAN YOU BE TRUSTED?

*Trustworthiness is the mark
of the true steward.*

Bob the Bible college student was taking a test. After cruising through a number of questions on the life of the Apostle Paul he came upon one that stopped him like a brick wall. "In 150 to 200 words, describe Paul's attitude toward Epaphroditus." Being the quick thinker that he was, Bob reasoned that Epaphroditus must have been Paul's physical ailment—the "thorn in the flesh" from which he suffered. And, because he knew how that problem had been so debilitating to Paul, Bob wrote an appropriately lengthy explanation!

Epaphroditus epitomized faithfulness and he understood that as stewards for Christ's sake we are co-workers, not competitors.

As Bob later learned to his chagrin, Epaphroditus was not a dreaded disease, but a dedicated disciple of Jesus Christ. In Paul's letter to the Philippians, he writes about this remarkable man, and the description is both encouraging and very convicting. Epaphroditus was above all a Christian who could be counted on. In any situation at any time, Paul knew that Epaphroditus would be true and reliable. Many of his so-called friends and co-workers had deserted Paul, but not Epaphroditus. He was a living example of the Principle of Faithful Giving that Paul taught to the Corinthians: "Now it is required that those who have been given a trust must prove faithful."[1] Another translation puts it this way: "Now what we look for in stewards is that they should be trustworthy."

Trustworthiness—faithful dependability—is the mark of the excellent steward. Epaphroditus epitomized this quality in all of his service for the Lord. In Philippians 2:25 he is described as a faithful worker, a faithful soldier and a faithful messenger. So deep was his commitment that he almost died for the work of Christ, risking his life to make up for the help the Philippians were unable to give to Paul. Epaphroditus understood perfectly that as stewards for Christ's sake we are co-workers, not competitors.

Christ-centered stewardship is the by-product of a Christ-like attitude. As Jesus told His disciples, "Those who are regarded as rulers of the Gentiles lord it over them, and their high officials exercise authority over them. Not so with you. Instead, whoever wants to become great among you must be your servant, and whoever wants to be first must be slave of all. For even the Son of Man did not come to be served, but to serve, and to give his life as a ransom for many."[2] The true steward is a true servant.

Faithful dependability as a Christian steward relates to the management of money, but also to a great deal more. The "portfolio" for which we are responsible includes a wide range of assets, and God's expectation is that we make the most of each one. Think of all the assets you have under management: your money, your time, your possessions, your opportunities, your influence, your relationships and much more. And to this long list can be added the spiritual assets with which we are entrusted: the Gospel of Christ, the mystery of godliness, the secret things of God. This is no small responsibility we bear, and to handle it rightly demands absolute faithfulness.

PRACTICING THE PRINCIPLES

In just about every one of Paul's epistles there is a clear statement about the priority of faithfulness. In the very first verse of Ephesians, he addresses "the saints in Ephesus, the *faithful* in Christ Jesus."[3] At the outset of Colossians, he writes, "To the holy and *faithful* brothers in Christ at Colosse."[4] To his spiritual son, Timothy, he repeatedly reinforced this same truth. And throughout the Bible we see that faithfulness is essential to serving God, to declaring His Word, to helping other believers and to handling situations of responsibility. From the Old Testament straight through the New, the wise, effective steward is shown to

The "portfolio" for which we are responsible includes a wide range of assets, and God's expectation is that we make the most of each one.

be utterly faithful. We see this virtue in Joseph when he was unjustly imprisoned. We observe it in Moses as he managed an entire nation in the middle of a wasteland. We find it in Daniel, who ran a government and could not be put down by his enemies, for "they could find no corruption in him, because he was trustworthy."[5] We see it in Epaphras whom Paul called "a *faithful* minister of Christ."[6]

To be a trustworthy steward, you must handle the small things with the same regard as the big things.

31

The Principle of Faithful Giving applies to the minor as well as the major things of life. Jesus said, "Whoever can be trusted with very little can also be trusted with much, and whoever is dishonest with very little will also be dishonest with much. So if you have not been trustworthy in handling worldly wealth, who will trust you with true riches? And if you have not been trustworthy with someone else's property, who will give you property of your own?"[7] The word is clear: the greater your dependability, the greater your blessing.

To be a trustworthy steward, you must see everything in life as sacred. For the believer, everything in life is sacred, and everything is to be devoted to the Lord. Whatever your talents, whatever your treasures, all are to be dedicated to God's purpose. "Whatever you do, do it all for the glory of God."[8]

Don't hoard the secret things of God; share them liberally. As a Christian, you are given access to what the Bible calls mysterious truth; but you're also given permission to share the secret. Tell it freely and eager-

ly, for no area of faithful dependability is more important than the stewardship of the Gospel.

Scripture References:
1 Corinthians 4:2
Mark 10:42-45
Ephesians 1:1
Colossians 1:2
Daniel 6:4
Colossians 1:7
Luke 16:10-12
1 Corinthians 10:31

5

ARE YOU A RIVER
OR A RESERVOIR?

*The richest generosity often comes
out of the deepest poverty.*

People are frequently confused about the difference between a paradox and an oxymoron. Both involve words which seem contradictory or incongruous. In the case of oxymorons, they're so interesting that "experts" faithfully record them. There's even a list of the Top 10 Oxymorons posted on several websites:

1. Government Organization

2. Same Difference

3. Taped Live

4. Plastic Glasses

5. Peace Force

6. Pretty Ugly

7. Head Butt

8. Working Vacation

9. Jumbo Shrimp

10. Tax Return

Oxymorons are intriguing and often down-right funny, but they are different from paradoxes. The main distinction is that a paradox, although it may appear opposed to common sense, is nevertheless true. The Christian life is full of paradoxes, and the teaching of Jesus was replete with them. For example, He taught that...

To find you must lose[1]

To be rich you must be poor[2]

To live you must die[3]

To be first you must be last[4]

To be honored you must be humbled[5]

And to this list we could add others. Suffice it to say that paradoxes were a major component of Jesus's teaching, as they were in the writings of the Apostle Paul. One important example is found in Paul's description of the Macedonian believers: "Out of the most severe trial, their overflowing joy and their extreme poverty welled up in rich generosity."[6] These exemplary Christians personified the Principle of Generous Giving, the spiritual law that says *the richest generosity often comes out of the deepest poverty.*

True generosity is not measured by the size of the gift but by the spirit of the giver, and the Macedonians had a joyous spirit which transcended their severe circumstances. They were a living

A paradox, although it may appear opposed to common sense, is never-theless true—and the Christian life is full of paradoxes.

God uses the simple things to confound the wise, and the little things to accomplish great deeds.

paradox: poor yet rich, pressed down yet rising up, humbled yet exalted. What a beautiful picture they were of the way believers should be. Their stewardship was exceptional, and it made an impact on others over a wide region.

The Principle of Generous Giving reminds us that God uses the simple things to confound the wise, and the little things to accomplish great deeds. He is not impressed with outward appearances or natural abilities because "the Lord looks upon the heart."[7] Some of the most effective servants of Jesus Christ have been the most unlikely men and women, people whose deepest longing was not to be known, but to make Him known. "Little is much if God is in it," says the well-known song, and it's true.

John Wesley was a paradox, the most unlikely leader of a major religious movement. A mere five feet four inches tall, he never weighed more than 120 pounds. As a child he was often sickly and at age six he nearly died when his home caught fire. But in his 88 years of life, spanning nearly the entire 18th century, he travelled more than a quarter million miles on horseback, preaching the Word and establishing churches. Along the way he delivered over 42,000 sermons and authored more than 200 books. He felt limited and inadequate, but he always found encouragement in God's promise: "I can do everything through him who gives me strength."[8] As a steward he was so efficient that upon his death, after his debts were paid, he left an estate of less than ten pounds! He had given away nearly everything he ever acquired, not wanting to hoard or hang onto anything. What a testimony of godly diligence, and what an inspiration to live by the Principle of Generous Giving.

PRACTICING THE PRINCIPLES

How shall we live by this important spiritual law? It comes down to several priorities:

Openness is willingness, and nothing pleases God more than a heart that willingly yields to Him and a hand that willingly gives to Him.

Respond to need, not to pressure. The generous giver is prompted to give by seeing a need and being touched by it. There may be an emotional element, but the primary motive is spiritual in nature. Giving is never to be done out of pressure or compulsion because it's a matter of grace, not law. We are to give because we want to give, love to give, and are grateful we can give.

Have an open heart and an open hand. Openness is willingness, and nothing pleases God more than a heart that willingly yields to Him and a hand that willingly gives to Him. If one claims to have an open heart but is not willing to have an open hand, something is amiss, for the two should be inseparable.

Be a river, not a reservoir. Believers are channels, not containers. God's love and grace are to flow through us, not be held in us. As stewards, our compelling desire must be to constantly give and give and give as the river of God's blessings courses through our lives.

Scripture References:
[1] Matthew 10:39
[2] Matthew 5:3
[3] Luke 17:33
[4] Matthew 19:30
[5] Matthew 23:12
[6] 2 Corinthians 8:2
[7] 1 Samuel 16:7
[8] Philippians 4:13

6

—GIVING GRATEFULLY—
WHAT ARE YOU THANKFUL FOR?

*Abundant grace brings abundant blessing
and spurs abundant ministry.*

At first glance they appeared to be just a pile of rocks. But their significance was great, for they represented God's blessing upon an entire nation. Joshua had instructed the people to carry twelve large stones from the bed of the Jordan River and place them on the Canaan side in a place called Gilgal. Arranged together, the stones formed a memorial to God's power in stopping the flow of the Jordan so that the people could cross over into the promised land. In subsequent years, the Israelites would periodically return to Gilgal to express their gratitude for victories won in their new land. On those important occasions they were to bring their children, so that no one would forget God's abundant grace upon them. Joshua said to them, "In the future, when your children ask you, 'What do these stones mean?' tell them that the flow of the Jordan was cut off before the ark of the covenant of the Lord. When it crossed the Jordan, the waters of the Jordan were cut off. These stones are to be a memorial to the people of Israel forever."[1]

Whenever the people of Israel obeyed God's instruction regarding the twelve stones, it provided a marvelous opportunity to instruct the next generation. A child's natural curiosity opens the door to describe God's remarkable power. And adults as well benefit from remembering what God has done. Recalling His abundant grace, the believer is encouraged and motivated to respond in worship and service. *God's abundant grace brings abundant blessing and spurs abundant ministry.* This is a basic principle of stewardship, the Principle of Grateful Giving. Paul explained it like this: "And God is able to make all grace abound to you, so that in all things at all times, having all that you need, you will abound in every good work."[2]

God's promise is limitless: He is able to make all grace abound toward us. His grace is relevant in all things at all times.

God's promise is limitless: He is able to make *all* grace abound toward us. His grace is relevant in *all* things at *all* times. He will provide *all* that we need. He will enable us to abound in *every* good work. There is no reason under any circumstances for us as believers to ever feel spiritually limited. Those two words alone—*all* and *every*—should be sufficient reminders of His power at work in us and for us.

If you want to be encouraged about God's power, look at the earthly ministry of Jesus. Consider the ways in which He transformed lives and remember

Communicating our gratitude to God is crucial because it makes us more reliant on the Lord.

that His power is still at work in us today. Think about the time that he encountered a demon-possessed man in the region of the Gerasenes. So tormented was the man that no one was able to subdue him, even with chains, and he spent night and day wandering among the tombs, crying out and cutting himself with sharp stones. Jesus asked him, "What is your name?" And the man replied, "My name is Legion, for we are many."[3] Actually, it was the numerous demons within the man replying. Jesus then cast out the demons, sending them into a herd of 2,000 pigs which promptly rushed into a nearby lake and drowned. The incident attracted much attention and people from the area came to see what had happened. "When they came to Jesus, they saw the man who had been possessed by the legion of demons, sitting there, dressed and in his right mind; and they were afraid."[4] A display of such spiritual power can be frightening, but its purpose is pure. Jesus told the man who had been set free from the demons, "Go home to your family and tell them how much the Lord has done for you, and how he has had mercy on you."[5]

Go and tell others how much the Lord has done for you. What a simple, powerful reminder this is to each of us to testify of all that God is doing in us. Private thanksgiving is important, but it is incomplete without a public acknowledgement of God's goodness. Communicating our gratitude to God is crucial because it makes us more reliant on the Lord and it has a profoundly positive effect on those around us. Thankfulness occurs inwardly, in what our heart expresses. Glorifying God happens publicly, in what our mouth confesses. Public expressions of gratitude for God's grace strengthen our commitment to Him while counteracting our human tendencies toward self-sufficiency and self-reliance. After all, our successes are not of our own making; they are the result of what God is doing in us and we are merely beneficiaries.

PRACTICING THE PRINCIPLES

We are stewards of God's abundant blessings, guardians of all that He has done and is doing in our lives.

We are stewards of God's abundant blessings, guardians of all that He has done and is doing in our lives. Our priority is to manage these unique resources with thankfulness and thoughtfulness.

Build a memorial of gratitude for God's grace. I'm not suggesting that you build an actual structure, but a written memorial of the ways in which God's abundant grace have resulted in abundant blessings in your life. The "stones" in your memorial are the great events and experiences through which God has taken you on your spiritual journey. As you remember each one, your appreciation will grow as your motivation in ministry grows.

Tell how much the Lord has done for you. You are the only steward of the story that only you can tell. No one else can give a first-person account of what God is doing to guide you, provide for you, empower you and bless you as you serve Him. Be a grateful giver by passing the word to others.

Scripture References:
[1] Joshua 4:6-7
[2] 2 Corinthians 9:8
[3] Mark 5:9
[4] Mark 5:15
[5] Mark 5:19

7

—GIVING HELPFULLY—
WHO'S ON FIRST
IN YOUR LIFE?

Through meeting others' needs
we meet our own.

The church is described by many metaphors in Scripture: It is called a flock[1], a vineyard[2], a temple[3], a family[4], a building[5] and a bride.[6] But most directly and specifically it is called a body.[7] As believers we are members of the body of Christ. We belong to Him and to one another in the most remarkable, most significant union. Like the members of a physical body, we the members of Christ's spiritual body serve a variety of purposes and fill a wide range of roles. As the Bible says, "The body is a unit, though it is made up

51

This was not communism but communion, the unfettered commitment of believers to one another, meeting needs and giving generously as they lived each day.

of many parts; and though all its parts are many, they form one body. So it is with Christ."[8]

As we relate to one another, there's no room for jealous comparison. "The eye cannot say to the hand, 'I don't need you!' And the head cannot say to the feet, 'I don't need you!' On the contrary, those parts of the body that seem to be weaker are indispensable, and the parts that we think are less honorable we treat with special honor."[9] This interconnectedness is a key element of biblical stewardship. It was the main concern when Paul wrote to the Corinthians, "Our desire is not that others might be relieved while you are hard pressed, but that there might be equality. At the present time, your plenty will supply what they need, so that in turn their plenty will supply what you need."[10] He was stating the vital Principle of Helpful Giving which teaches us that *through meeting others' needs we meet our own.*

From the earliest days of the Church, this principle was in effect. Acts chapter 2 describes how it worked among the first Christians: "All the believers were together and had everything in common. Selling their possessions and goods, they gave to anyone as he had need."[11] This was not communism but communion—the unfettered commitment of believers to one another, meeting needs and giving generously as they together met the challenges of each day. Each person was exercising his or her gifts for the greater benefit of the body. They were reciprocating, which according to *Webster's*, is "giving and taking mutually."

The importance of spiritual gifts must not be underestimated because without them we cannot function properly in Christ's body. A spiritual gift is a divinely ordained ability through which Christ enables His Church to accomplish its purposes on earth. In short, it is a Spirit-given capacity for Christian service.

A spiritual gift is a divinely ordained ability through which Christ enables His Church to accomplish its purposes on earth.

The source of each gift is God Himself, and the nature of each gift is purely spiritual. It is not a talent, for talents have to do with natural abilities. Talents instruct, inspire or entertain on a natural level; but spiritual gifts are for service, ministry and edification. Talents and gifts may be related, but they are not one and the same. For example, a person who is naturally visionary may be given the gift of faith. A natural teacher may be given the gift of teaching. These are merely possibilities; the actual giving of spiritual gifts is determined by God alone.

A. B. Simpson, founder of the Christian & Missionary Alliance, observed seven principles pertaining to spiritual gifts. We are wise to remember them:

1. Every believer has some gift, therefore all should be encouraged.

2. No one has all the gifts, therefore all should be humble.

3. All gifts are for the Body, therefore all should be harmonious.

4. All gifts are for the Lord, therefore all should be contented.

5. All gifts are mutually helpful, therefore all should be faithful.

6. All gifts promote the whole Body's health, therefore none can be dispensed with.

7. All gifts depend upon the Holy Spirit's empowerment, therefore none should be out of fellowship with Him.

PRACTICING THE PRINCIPLES

One fact that we keep coming back to is that Christian stewardship is not fulfilled in a vacuum. It is not merely an individual responsibility, for we belong to one another and must think of one another, not just ourselves. To live by the Principle of Helpful Giving is to maintain an upward and outward attitude, not an inward focus. There's a memorable children's song that says it simply and brilliantly:

> *Jesus and Others and You,*
> *what a wonderful way to spell JOY.*
> *Jesus and Others and You,*
> *in the life of each girl and each boy.*
> *J is for Jesus, who died in our place;*
> *O is for Others we know face to face;*
> *Y is for You, and whatever you do,*
> *Put yourself last to spell JOY.*

This is how we demonstrate true helpfulness and this how we experience real joy—serving the Lord and caring for others as faithful stewards.

When you face a big need, try to find someone else with that same need. Pray for them, help them, and do everything in your ability to meet their need. Focus your interest and care on others, and rely upon the

Lord to meet your needs and bless your service. Put the principle of reciprocity to work and see what God will do.

Use your gifts. Giving monetary gifts is important and needful, but giving ministry gifts in service for Christ is vital. Know your giftedness and use it for God's glory.

Look constantly for Body-building opportunities. Of course, I'm referring to building up the spiritual body, the Body of Christ; and the way this happens is through ministry to one another. We are to forbear one another[12], forgive one another[13], submit to one another[14], admonish one another[15], comfort one another[16] and exhort one another.[17] By doing these things, we grow spiritually stronger and healthier.

Scripture References:
[1] John 10:1-15, 26-30
[2] John 15:1-10
[3] Romans 14:17
[4] Ephesians 2:19
[5] Ephesians 2:20-22
[6] Ephesians 5:22-32

Scripture References (cont.):

[7] 1 Corinthians 12:12-27
[8] 1 Corinthians 12:12
[9] 1 Corinthians 12:21-23
[10] 2 Corinthians 8:13-14
[11] Acts 2:44-45
[12] Ephesians 4:2
[13] Colossians 3:13
[14] Ephesians 5:21
[15] Colossians 3:16
[16] 1 Thessalonians 4:18
[17] Hebrews 3:13

8

DOES GIVING MAKE YOU HAPPY?

*God loves the giver
who gives with a happy heart.*

The scene was really nothing to laugh about, but it unleashed howls of delight, caused several fender-benders and brought traffic to a screeching halt on a busy freeway. People were literally jumping from their cars and rushing to grab the loot—several hundred thousand dollars worth—that was flying out the back door of an armored truck. The driver had failed to lock the door and the money was sucked out as if being removed by a giant vacuum. Even after the police arrived it took quite a while for order to be restored, and much of the money was never recovered.

The security guard failed to be diligent, and it cost him his job. Chances are he never imagined so many strangers would take advantage of his foolish misfortune. His experience reminds us that there are several forms of generosity. In the case of the flying funds, the generosity was completely unintentional. Sometimes, generosity is reluctant, particularly when one feels pressured to give. Generosity can also be manipulative, especially in situations where a gift is given for some ulterior motive. And it's not uncommon for generosity to be self-serving when one gives to gain some attention or advantage. In stark contrast, biblical generosity is like none of these. It is intentional, not the least bit reluctant, not manipulative and definitely not self-serving. Above all, it is full of joy. As the Apostle Paul explained, it is prompted by what one "has decided in his heart to give, not reluctantly or under compulsion, for God loves a cheerful giver."[1]

Herein is one of the most important principles for balanced Christian living, the Principle of Hilarious Giving. The word translated as "cheerful" in most English Bibles literally means "hilarious." It carries the idea of one who is uproariously delighted to give. Not grudgingly, like some sort of scrooge or miser, but freely

The word translated as "cheerful" in most English Bibles means "hilarious." It carries the idea of one who is uproariously delighted to give.

and openly and happily. It's the absolute opposite of one who gives to God because he feels he can't refuse to give, or because someone else is giving and it would reflect poorly on him if he didn't give. Living by the Principle of Hilarious Giving, one does not give under the whiplash of necessity, complaining inwardly or being bitter in any way. Rather, one is thankful to even be able to give.

The hilarious giver remembers that Christ was infinitely rich yet for our sake became poor, laying

God loves a cheerful giver because it is the right and honorable response to the greatness of His own gifts to His children.

aside the glory He had with the Father. With such an example of selfless giving, why would one not give cheerfully in return? God loves a cheerful giver because it is the right and honorable response to the greatness of His own giving. How could God feel in any way drawn toward a Christian who is willing that Heaven be bankrupted on his behalf then give as little as possible in return? The answer is, He isn't drawn to such a person.

Think of all the reasons to give with hilarious generosity: God, with a heart full of perfect love and compassion, gave His only Son to purchase our salvation. He gave the Holy Spirit as our eternal comforter, guide and teacher. He gave us the promise of life abundant here and life forever with Him in Heaven. He gave free access into His presence, allowing us to come with our petitions, and promising to hear and answer when we pray. He gave all this and so much more! How can we not give?

PRACTICING THE PRINCIPLES

When one gives with hilarious generosity, there is a conscious recognition of being a channel of blessings. We are passing on what He has passed to us. Imagine the feelings of the disciples when Jesus took those five loaves of bread and two fish and turned them into a feast for thousands. Think of the hilarious joy they felt in handing out food to the hungry, seeing God multiply it as long as they kept sharing.[2] What a beautiful picture of what it's like for us when we give from the endless resources He entrusts to us.

God does not promise to solve all our problems, but He does promise to supply all our needs. The Bible assures us that "God will meet all your needs according to his glorious riches in Christ Jesus."[3] And, with our needs met, what more can we ask, and what more can we do than to give in return. He is "able to make all grace abound to you, so that in all things at all times, having all that you need, you will abound in every good work."[4] His purpose is that we serve Him fully and that we give hilariously in the process.

Keep in mind these practical perspectives for hilarious givers:

Don't talk yourself out of giving. Whenever you have a good opportunity to give, take it. In fact, look for opportunities to give generously, and live with an eager anticipation of how God will use you to bless others and please Him.

Take money seriously, but not too seriously. As Proverbs cautions, "Don't wear yourself out to get rich."[5] Money is important, but it isn't everything, and it can't bring true satisfaction. If you take money too seriously it can cloud your judgment and alter your motives. The generous giver remembers that money is a means to an end, not the end itself.

Give with a smile, not a cringe. When one gives with hilarious generosity, it's only natural to smile.

After all, God's desire is not that we go through life simply collecting things and holding on to them. Instead, He wants us to give and give and give, just as He Himself does.

Scripture References:
[1] 2 Corinthians 9:7
[2] Mark 6:32-44
[3] Philippians 4:19
[4] 2 Corinthians 9:8
[5] Proverbs 23:4

9

—GIVING HONORABLY—
ARE YOU AN OWNER OR A STEWARD?

*Nothing truly belongs to us;
everything actually belongs to God.*

Perspective governs life in remarkable ways. Consider the story of the blind man who attempted to describe an elephant. He put his arms around one of the animal's massive legs and said, "the bark is very rough." He felt the tusk and said, "the branches are smooth but strong." Finally, he handled the giant ear and remarked, "the elephant's leaves are huge and thick." In conclusion he declared, "the elephant is one of the world's most unusual trees."

Lest we laugh at the blind man's mispercep-
tion, let's remember that we too can get things very
wrong at times. Even those of us who have learned
that God owns everything often act as if He really
doesn't. An indisputable law of stewardship is that
*Nothing truly belongs to us; everything actually belongs
to God.* King David acknowledged this when he stated
categorically: "everything in heaven and earth is
yours, O Lord." And he adds right after that statement, "wealth and honor come from you; you are the
ruler of all things."[1]

When we are blessed with money and material things, and when we receive acclaim for any accom-
plishment, we're getting not what we deserve but
what God in His grace lovingly allows us to enjoy and
to care for. The essence of life is not ownership but
stewardship—the faithful management of all that God
entrusts to us. Some of us are entrusted with a lot,
some with a little; but whatever comes to us brings
with it an undeniable responsibility. The temptation is

to think that abundance is found in possessing life's benefits, when actually it's discovered in stewarding life's blessings. That's why Jesus warned His disciples: "Be on your guard against all kinds of greed, for a man's life does not consist in the abundance of his possessions."[2] There is only one rightful owner, and true

When we give with the right motive and the right focus we are living by the Principle of Honorable Giving— our gifts honor God and give Him pleasure.

satisfaction comes to us only in acknowledging Him and wisely managing His resources. When we give with the right motive and the right focus we are living by the Principle of Honorable Giving—our gifts honor God and give Him pleasure.

In what ways can we put this truth into practice? Obviously this is a tough task since the stewardship mindset is so at odds with the prevailing North American attitude of ownership. Nearly everyone falls prey to the notion that life is more fulfilling if we simply have more things. Under the constant barrage of advertisements and appeals it's easy to give in to the belief that we deserve everything we can get. But it's not true, and we run a major risk when we look at life in terms of *our* things, *our* money, *our* possessions, *our* abilities, *our* opinions or *our* achievements. As the Bible says, "we brought nothing into this world, and it is certain we can carry nothing out."[3] You'll never see a hearse pulling a U-Haul trailer.

At the height of his power, John D. Rockefeller, America's first oil baron, was the richest man in the world. In the early years of the 20th century, his businesses accounted for one of every thirty dollars generated in the entire U.S. economy. In today's currency that would be equal to a fortune ten times greater than Bill Gates has amassed. When Rockefeller died in 1937 a newspaper artist drew a cartoon which posed the question, "How much did he leave?" The answer in the next panel said simply, "He left it all." And that's the way it is for everyone. At the moment of death, every "possession" of this material life is left behind—even the bodies we once inhabited. Only the spirit lives on, for only the spirit is eternal.

The "real" reality is found not in the physical world, but the spiritual. That's why Paul told Timothy that "physical exercise is of some value, but godliness has value for all things, holding promise for both the present life and the life to come."[4] Understanding the "real" reality, the Christian steward is able to see life from God's perspective, setting affections and attentions on an entirely different realm—the spiritual realm.

PRACTICING THE PRINCIPLES

As you endeavor to give honorably—giving for God's honor and His glory—let your thinking be guided by three priorities:

Think of yourself as the manager of a trust. You have been given a key role and a great responsibility, so make the most of it. God Himself has entrusted you with time, money, material things and great

God Himself has entrusted you with time, money, material things and great opportunities.

opportunities. Your objective is to maximize the investment of all that has been put into your hands.

Think of each day as an opportunity for service and stewardship. Time is a precious commodity and we have a limited allotment of days, hours and minutes. Ephesians 5:15-16 advises, "Be very careful, then, how you live—not as unwise but as wise, making the most of every opportunity." It's similar to the popular motto, *carpe diem*, the Latin admonition to "seize the day." But the believer's motto is actually "seize the day for God." In other words, live every day expressly for His glory and His purposes.

Think of money as a means to an end, not the end itself. The allure of money is strong and pervasive. It permeates our frantic, workaholic culture; but it brings no lasting fulfillment. It always creates a thirst for more, unless one has the right attitude toward it and determines to manage it rather than be manipulated by it. In the final analysis, the hallmark of stewardship is administration, not acquisition. Only by pursuing the goal of pleasing God do we find true pleasure and satisfaction for ourselves.

Scripture References:
[1] 1 Chronicles 29:11
[2] Luke 12:15
[3] 1 Timothy 6:7
[4] 1 Timothy 4:8

10

—GIVING JOYFULLY—
GOT SATISFACTION?

*Wise stewards are happy with what they have,
not harried by what they don't have.*

Prisons today are five-star resorts compared to those
in which Paul languished. He didn't have a heated cell
with a private toilet and sink. There was no mattress
on which to sleep, no TV room in which to relax, no
well-stocked library for reading and study. There was
only the dark encasement of roughly hewn stones,
damp air filled with putrid odors and the pungent
reminders of human depravity. Perhaps worst of all
were the chains, their rusty coarseness scraping his
skin raw, constantly tugging at him.

As if imprisonment were not painful enough, Paul had to endure the stinging criticism of those who called themselves his Christian brothers.

And, as if imprisonment were not painful enough, Paul had to endure the stinging criticism of those who called themselves his Christian brothers. They dared to attack God's apostle even while he was held captive.

Stop and imagine yourself in Paul's situation. Feel the weight of the chains on raw skin. Taste the nauseating swill that was his daily food. Listen to those dreadful sounds of suffering that filled his ears day and night. Look into the menacing eyes of the Roman prison guards.

You are there. You are suffering. You are chained. You are Paul the apostle. Now, what's your attitude? What fills your heart through the weary hours? Here's what Paul wrote to his friends in Philippi: "Now I want you to know, brothers, that what has happened to me has really served to advance the gospel. As a result, it has become clear throughout the whole palace guard and to everyone else that I am in chains for Christ. Because of my chains, most of the brothers in the Lord have been encouraged to speak the word of God more courageously and fearlessly."[1]

What an attitude! Rather than being inflamed with furious self-pity, Paul is encouraged by the positive impact of his negative condition. In spite of the severity, he is joyful. What a lesson he teaches us! We have troubles and trials, sure; but what is our attitude, and what is our commitment? Paul kept going because he lived by the Principle of Joyful Giving. He knew that he was just a pilgrim, and his affections were directed above, not below. From personal experience he could tell his brothers and sisters in Christ, "Set your minds on things above, not on earthly things."[2]

Wise stewards are happy with what they have, not harried by what they don't have. "Godliness with contentment is great gain," Paul wrote in a letter to

Timothy, "for we brought nothing into the world, and we can take nothing out of it."[3] When each of us arrives in our birthday suit we have nothing but a physical body. And, although we amass things throughout life, when we depart this world we leave everything behind. Our properties, our vehicles, our furnishings, our bank accounts, the clothes in our closets—it's all left behind. When the moment of our departure comes—as it certainly will—all that matters is what we've built up in spiritual riches.

PRACTICING THE PRINCIPLES

Be satisfied with life's essentials. It's easy in a culture of abundance to define "essentials" in a much broader sense than God ever intended. We should in fact think as simply as possible, being willing to be satisfied with food to eat, clothes to wear, and a place to live. For Paul, the essentials were even fewer. He wrote: "But if we have food and clothing, we will be content with that."[4] Being satisfied is not a struggle if one simply remembers the goodness of God. As the psalmist said, "He satisfies your desires with good things."[5]

Being satisfied is not a struggle if one simply remembers the goodness of God.

Be wary of life's temptations. One of life's biggest temptations is money. We all want it, and most of us want a lot of it. But, as the Scripture reminds us, "the love of money is a root of all kinds of evil."[6] It can sidetrack us from God's core purposes and make us forget that His indwelling presence is our source. "Keep your lives free from the love of money and be content with what you have, because God has said, 'Never will I leave you; never will I forsake you.' So we say with confidence, 'The Lord is my helper; I will not be afraid. What can man do to me?'"[7]

Be happy in life's circumstances. Circumstances change constantly. We can go from delight to disaster in a single day. For the faith-filled believer, it really doesn't matter how things are going because confidence in the Lord transcends concern for the circum-stances. Paul wrote from prison, "I have learned to be content whatever the circumstances. I know what it is to be in need, and I know what it is to have plenty. I have learned the secret of being content in any and every situation, whether well fed or hungry, whether living in plenty or in want."[8] The "secret" that Paul learned is that Christ enables us to be happy regard-less of what is going on. He is the constant in a world of change. Through His empowerment we can live by the Principle of Joyful Giving.

Scripture References:
[1] Philippians 1:12-14
[2] Colossians 3:2
[3] 1 Timothy 6:6-7
[4] 1 Timothy 6:8
[5] Psalm 103:5
[6] 1 Timothy 6:10
[7] Hebrews 13:6
[8] Philippians 4:11-12

11

—GIVING PROPORTIONATELY—
ARE YOU GIVING
YOUR FAIR SHARE?

*God's provision dictates the believer's
proportion.*

The images are painfully familiar: hollow-cheeked mothers, their faces etched with despair, children with distended stomachs, desperate people dying of malnutrition. Whenever we see such dreadful sights, we feel a stirring of compassion for those who suffer and we long to help in some way. At the same time, we're reminded that dire circumstances have plagued mankind throughout history. Jesus said that the poor would be with us always, and He declared that the priority, regardless of one's lot in life, is to glorify God

As Jesus loved without limits and gave without restriction, so are we to do in proportion to His provision for us.

and trust Him explicitly. Whatever the situation, whatever the limitations, we are to worship and serve the Lord wholeheartedly. Just as Jesus loved without limits and gave without restriction, so are we to love and give in proportion to His provision for us.

Genuine worship is characterized by genuine faith, and sometimes that faith must be proven in the face of extreme conditions. Let's take a look at two examples, one from Old Testament days and the other from the New Testament era.

In 1 Kings 17 we read of a widow from the region called Zarephath. Not only was she without a husband, she also had no observable resources except a few ounces of oil and a handful of flour. The circumstances were severe because a three-year drought had devastated Israel, due to the people's disobedience to

God. Elijah the prophet, trusting in God to provide his daily bread, was instructed by the Lord to go to the widow for his supply. When he arrived, she was gathering sticks to build the fire for her final supper, since she had enough for only one more meal for herself and her son. She was resigned to starve to death.

Elijah asked the widow for water, then for a piece of bread. She then explained her circumstances, and Elijah did what seems to be irrational and even ridiculous to the natural mind. He told her to not fear, but to make him a small cake, and then make one for her son. Then he promised her that she would have sufficient supply until the rains were restored.

She obeyed, and God fulfilled His word. Facing death, both Elijah and the widow were responding to specific instructions from the Lord, not wild suppositions. For him to make such a request would take great faith. For her to simply respond demonstrated an authentic, sacrificial act of worship. When she engaged with God according to His terms and in the way He established, God's work continued and her needs were amply and miraculously provided for. By an act of her will she took the leap of faith and gave what she was trusting in to sustain her life, if even for just a little while.[1]

The essential purpose of this story is to remind us that giving is an integral act of worship. The widow gave something out of her own need. She gave first to sustain the work of the Lord and fulfill the word of the Lord. God then opened his windows of grace and miraculously multiplied her gift—and the divine supply came for at least one full year.

Now let's turn our attention to a group of believers who lived several centuries later in the region of Macedonia. As we've already seen in previous chapters, Paul says some interesting things about these brothers and sisters in Christ. He wrote to the Corinthians: "And now, brothers, we want you to know about the grace that God has given the Macedonian churches. Out of the most severe trial, their overflowing joy and their extreme poverty welled up in rich generosity. For I testify that they gave as much as they were able, and even beyond their ability. Entirely on their own, they urgently pleaded with us for the privilege of

The Macedonians were persecuted severely and materially poor, yet spiritually they lived above it all.

sharing in this service to the saints. And they did not do as we expected, but they gave themselves first to the Lord and then to us in keeping with God's will."[2]

The young churches of Macedonia were persecuted severely and were materially poor, yet spiritually they lived above the extreme conditions and excelled in giving it their all. Specifically, they gave to a ministry project that the Apostle Paul had initiated; and they gave in a most remarkable way: sacrificially, beyond their ability, willingly and eagerly—of themselves to God and of their resources to God's work.

The Principle of Proportionate Giving—a

powerful law of stewardship—is evident both in the widow of Zarephath and the Christians of Macedonia. This principle teaches us that *God's provision dictates the believer's proportion.* In other words, what He provides determines what we give. If He gives a little, from that little we are to give; if He gives abundantly, from that abundance we are to give. Whatever He provides, regardless of the depth or breadth, determines the measure of our giving. As Jesus reminded His disciples, "To whom much is given, much is required."[3]

PRACTICING THE PRINCIPLES

Don't worry about what you have or don't have to give. The Principle of Proportionate Giving is a reassuring truth of Scripture because it eliminates the pressure of thinking about what we have or don't have to give. Relying upon the Lord and depending upon Him as our source, we grow in grace as we give. In the process, giving becomes a therapeutic experience, for as we die to self we come alive in faith.

Give in proportion to everything you have received. Proportionate participation in the work of God involves much more than money. Whatever God has given you, in whatever measure, is to be dedicated to him. Your talents, your abilities, your material wealth, your time—all are resources from which you can give.

Deny the dominance of worldly thinking. Worldly attitudes emphasize *me* and *mine*, and they can suck us into a whirlpool of obsessions. John the Apostle cautioned, "Do not love the world or anything in the world. If anyone loves the world, the love of the Father is not in him."[4] As believers in Jesus Christ, we belong to a different universe. Our citizenship is in heaven, and if we act as if our citizenship is in this corrupt world, we lose sight and we lose the fullness of God's blessing.

God will provide. That's a certainty. And the proportion of His provision defines the proportion of our giving.

Scripture References:
[1] 1 Kings 17:2-24
[2] 2 Corinthians 8:1-5
[3] Luke 12:48
[4] 1 John 2:15

12

—GIVING PURPOSEFULLY—
HAVE YOU DISCOVERED THE PURPOSE OF PROSPERITY?

*We are made rich in every way
to be generous on every occasion.*

The year was 1903. Theodore Roosevelt ruled with a strong hand as President of the United States. Master engineers had launched a massive project to link the oceans by digging a great canal through the Isthmus of Panama. Henry Ford was tinkering with his newest invention, the Model T automobile. Two brothers from Ohio, Orville and Wilbur Wright, had just achieved the first successful flight of an airplane. It was an era of innovation, an age of breathtaking

He decided to give up all the pleasures of his position, all the advantages at his disposal. In his Bible he wrote two words: No Reserves.

advancement. The future was brimming with promise, especially for William Borden, a bright young high school graduate from Chicago.

William was an unusual teenager, most notably because he was a millionaire. As heir to the Borden Dairy fortune, life was rich with possibilities and the world was his to discover. In fact, that is literally what young Bill did after his graduation—he discovered the world, travelling around the globe for an entire year. He encountered foreign cultures and explored intriguing places; and everywhere he went he was touched by the desperate needs of people. In a letter to his parents he announced his intentions to devote his life to missionary service. In effect, he had decided to give up all the pleasures of his position, all the advantages at his disposal. In his Bible he wrote two words: No Reserves.

In the fall of 1905, William Borden enrolled at Yale University. One of his classmates later wrote of him: "He came to college far ahead spiritually of any of us. We who were his classmates learned to lean on him and find in him a strength that was solid as a rock, just because of his settled purpose and consecration." At Yale, Borden was not only an exceptional student but a gifted leader, personally spearheading a movement of spiritual renewal on the campus. So powerful was the movement that, by his senior year, over 1,000 of Yale's 1,300 students were attending weekly Bible fellowships. Off campus, Borden was active as well, rescuing down-and-outers and drunks from the streets of New Haven. He established the Yale Hope Mission to give them a place of refuge and rehabilitation.

Upon his graduation from Yale, William could have moved directly into the huge family business or taken any of numerous job offers. But his intentions to become a missionary never wavered. For him, there remained only one more stage of preparation, a course of theological studies at Princeton Seminary, which he completed in two years. After receiving his degree, William was ready to take the boldest step of all: a one-way trip to Egypt. There he would learn Arabic in order to reach Muslims with the Gospel. Leaving family and fortune behind, he set sail across the Atlantic. On the way, he wrote two more words in his Bible: No Retreats.

William arrived in Cairo full of anticipation and ready for the challenge. With customary zeal he immersed himself in the task at hand; but within days he became very weak. He had been stricken with spinal meningitis, and it was a force he could not withstand. A short time later, William Whiting Borden died at the age of 25.

When the news of William's death was cabled from Egypt, tears flowed and hearts ached an ocean away. One biographer wrote, "It seemed as though a wave of sorrow went round the world...for William Borden not only gave his wealth, but himself, in a way so joyous and natural that it was manifestly a privilege rather than a sacrifice." In terms of human logic, the death of such a promising young man was a waste. But that was not William's perspective. During the last fleeting days of his life, in labored handwriting, he had penned two more words in his Bible: No Regrets.

The legacy of William Borden can be summed up in those six poignant words he recorded so deliberately: No Reserves. No Retreats. No Regrets. He had taken to heart the incontrovertible truths of biblical stewardship which were written down by another missionary, the Apostle Paul, many centuries before. One of those truths is the Principle of Purposeful Giving, which Paul expressed in his second letter to the believers in Corinth: "Now he who supplies seed to the sower and bread for food will also supply and increase your store of seed and will enlarge the harvest of your righteousness. You will be made rich in every way so that you can be generous on every occasion."[1] Examine these words closely and you'll see a promise coupled with a purpose. The promise—"You will be made rich in every way"—is an assurance of abundant giving, the certainty that God will provide you with everything you need. The purpose—"So that you can be generous on every occasion"—is an encouragement to abundant generosity, cheerfully and willingly giving to others in response to God's gifts to you.

William Borden, though just a young man, had learned well the Principle of Purposeful Giving. He took full advantage of every way in which he had been made rich in order to show generosity to others at every opportunity. Everything in his life—indeed, life itself—he had dedicated to the Savior. William Borden did not live a long life, but he lived a full life—full of hope, full of grace, full of faith and full of love for God and others.

PRACTICING THE PRINCIPLES

Giving on purpose begins with living on purpose. The purpose of your life should be the basis and motivating force behind your giving. If your life purpose is to honor God and serve Him wholeheartedly, everything you give—whether it is money, time, energy, influence or some other gift—is to be an expression of that foundational purpose. There should be no conflict between why you live and why you give: they are part and parcel of a Christ-centered continuum. If any other motivations worm their way into your heart, and if you give in to those motivations, you will lose the joy and the blessing. When you write a check to your church, for example, don't think about the benefits of tax deductibility; think about God's blessings which enable you both to live and to give.

Blessing others generously is a delight, not a duty. Many Christians trudge through life burdened down by an inordinate sense of duty. They've been taught that God demands full obedience and compliance with His laws, which is absolutely true; but they've been taught in a way that binds rather than frees. They have a view of God that leaves them emotionally restricted instead of spiritually free. Christian obedience is not an oppressive, burdensome thing. It is the joyous response of a grateful heart. Likewise, Christian generosity is the natural expression of one who purpose-fully blesses others. It is a delight, not a duty.

Stewardship is measured qualitatively, not just quantitatively. Some would argue that William Borden could have been a more effective steward if he had used his great wealth to underwrite Christian ministry. They would question whether it was really logical for him to take such a rough path when a smooth road was so readily available. However, what matters most to God is not our logic but our love—the love that denies self, takes up the cross and follows Him unreservedly. This is what Jesus was talking about when he told a rich young man of the ruling class to sell everything he had and give it all to the poor. Unfortunately, the young man was not willing to take such a drastic step because he loved his posses-sions more than he loved God. Christian stewardship is first and foremost a qualitative matter of the heart, not a quantitative measurement of one's gifts.

Scripture Reference:
[1] 2 Corinthians 9:11

13

WHAT HAVE YOU BEEN GIVEN?

*Those who receive great blessing
are to respond with great giving.*

T his is a tale of two offerings.

Both offerings were for the purpose of funding the construction of extraordinary places of worship—a grand Tabernacle and a great Temple.

Both offerings were taken by extraordinary men of God—one by Moses, the other by King David.

Both offerings required the extraordinary involvement of God's people giving of their money,

The people gave so much that their response created an unheard-of "crisis" and Moses had to intervene.

their time, their skills, their possessions and their energy.

These two offerings were given under very different circumstances by people who lived in different eras, hundreds of years apart. But the similarities are striking, especially in the wholehearted response to a formidable challenge.

The first offering, given by the nation of Israel for the building of the Tabernacle, was utterly unique. No project like it had ever been done in the annals of human history, and the architect was none other than God Himself, who revealed the plans to the prophet Moses. Everything about the Tabernacle was distinctive: exotic woods, spectacular fabrics, elaborately symbolic furnishings, even special garments for the priests to wear while inside the structure. Building it was a demanding, complex task. But the people rose to the occasion: "Then Moses summoned...every skilled person to whom the Lord had given ability and who was willing to come and do the work. They received from Moses all the offerings the Israelites had brought to carry out the work of constructing the sanctuary. And the people continued to bring freewill offerings morning after morning."[1]

The people were giving and giving, so much in fact that their response was overwhelming: "So all the skilled craftsmen who were doing all the work on the sanctuary left their work and said to Moses, 'The people are bringing more than enough for doing the work the Lord commanded to be done.'"[2] That's right: they gave more than was needed! It was an unheard-of "crisis" and Moses had to intervene: "Then Moses gave an order and they sent this word throughout the camp: 'No man or woman is to make anything else as an offering for the sanctuary.' And so the people were restrained from bringing more, because what they already had was more than enough to do all the work."[3]

Imagine a pastor today having to say, "Please don't give any more to the building fund. You've already given more than we need." It's doubtful that we'll ever hear those words, and it underscores what a phenomenal response the people of Israel made.

In the offering received by King David, the project was different yet nonetheless distinctive. In fact, it was the most captivatingly beautiful building ever to be constructed, a palatial structure dedicated to God. David personally set the example in giving to the offering: "With all my resources I have provided for the temple of my God—gold for the gold work, silver for the silver, bronze for the bronze, iron for the iron and wood for the wood, as well as onyx for the settings, turquoise, stones of various colors, and all kinds of fine stone and marble—all of these in large quantities." And he wasn't done, even with that extravagant generosity. "Besides," he said, "in my devotion to the temple of my God I now give my personal treasures of gold and silver for the temple of my

God, over and above everything I have provided for this holy temple."[4] David, being the inspirational and God-honoring leader he was, demonstrated the importance of the offering by giving superabundantly—an "over and above" contribution.

Imagine a pastor today having to say, "Please don't give any more to the building fund. You've already given more than we need."

The people of Israel, inspired by their king's example, gave with great enthusiasm, joyously expressing their commitment. David put it all in perspective: "O Lord our God, as for all this abundance that we have provided for building you a temple for your Holy Name, it comes from your hand, and all of it belongs to you. I know, my God, that you test the heart and are pleased with integrity. All these things have I given willingly and with honest intent. And now I have seen with joy how willingly your people who are here have given to you."[5]

We can learn much from the generosity of God's people who gave for the Tabernacle and the Temple.

Two offerings, given by different people in different eras, yet similar in many ways. Both are examples of the Principle of Responsive Giving, the precept which teaches us that *those who receive great blessing are to respond with great giving.* Even though they lived so long ago, we can learn much from the generosity of God's people who participated in the offerings for the Tabernacle and the Temple. Their obedience is exemplary, and we are wise to replicate it in our experience as believers of the 21st century. Here are some ways we can do that:

PRACTICING THE PRINCIPLES

When your church has a major project, get involved in a major way. The contribution of your money is important, of course; but equally valuable (to you and to the church) is the contribution of your unique talents and abilities. Whatever you have to offer, be it money, goods, professional skills or practical advice, be willing to participate in a major way.

When you give to the Lord's work, go above and beyond the call of duty. Don't be a "status quo" Christian, content to simply do and give what's expected. Expand the horizons of your faith and go above and beyond in your giving to the Lord.

When you receive a challenge to give, see it as an opportunity, not an interference. Everything comes from God's hand and it all belongs to Him anyway, so how could we see giving as anything but a great opportunity? Let's make David's prayer our own: "O Lord...keep this desire in the hearts of your people forever, and keep their hearts loyal to you."[6]

Scripture References:
[1] Exodus 36:2-3
[2] Exodus 36:4-5
[3] Exodus 36:6-7
[4] 1 Chronicles 29:2-3
[5] 1 Chronicles 29:16-17
[6] 1 Chronicles 29:18

14

—GIVING SACRIFICIALLY—
WHAT ARE YOU GIVING UP?
*The most significant gifts are often given
by the most unlikely givers.*

He sat down opposite the collection area and watched intently as the offerings were given. People from all walks of life were entering the courtyard to make their contributions to the temple treasury. Among the crowd were a number of rich people who threw in large amounts of money. Undoubtedly some gave with a flourish that drew attention to their great generosity. But then He spotted her, a lowly widow who entered humbly and put in two very small copper coins, worth only a fraction of a penny. Calling His disciples to him, Jesus said, "I tell you the truth, this

It's doubtful that anyone but Jesus noticed her that day, but God is paying attention and He sees things that no one else sees.

poor widow has put more into the treasury than all the others. They gave out of their wealth; but she, out of her poverty, put in everything—all she had to live on."[1]

Everyone else had given out of their abundance, but she gave her all. In one simple act she demonstrated true sacrifice, proven not just by what she put in, but by what she had left over. She epitomized the Principle of Sacrificial Giving, showing that *the most significant gifts are often given by the most unlikely givers.* It's doubtful that anyone but Jesus actually noticed her that day, but God is paying attention and He sees things no one else sees and interprets meaning no one else grasps. What matters to Him is wholehearted devotion, and what pleases Him is the exercise of genuine faith. The poor widow was wholly devoted to God, willing by faith to give everything. She loved the Lord with an absolute love, and He would bless her abundantly for that consecration to Him.

What God desires of us as stewards is that we live by a philosophy of life that reflects His character. Jesus gave a potent illustration of this when He was asked by a young Jewish lawyer, "Teacher, what must I do to inherit eternal life?" Jesus answered with a question of His own: "What is written in the Law? How do you read it?" The lawyer replied, quoting Scripture: "Love the Lord your God with all your heart and with all your soul and with all your strength and with all your mind, and Love your neighbor as yourself." To this, Jesus said, "You have answered correctly. Do this and you will live." But the man wasn't satisfied with Jesus' answer, and he asked, "And who is my neighbor?"[2] In reply, Jesus told a story that is among the best known of all His teachings, the parable of the Good Samaritan.[3] In that unforgettable account, Jesus reveals three essential philosophies of life:

The first philosophy says, *"What's yours is mine."*

The second says, *"What's mine is mine."*

The third philosophy expresses the belief that *"What's mine is yours."*

The first philosophy—*What's Yours is Mine*—is shown through the behavior of thieves who attack a defenseless man on the road to Jericho. They beat him mercilessly, strip off his clothing, steal all his belongings and leave him naked and bleeding at the roadside.

A short time later, two "religious" men, a priest and a Levite, happen to walk by the scene of the crime. However, they do nothing to help. In fact, they cross the road to avoid getting any closer. Their philosophy—*What's Mine is Mine*—dictates that they mind their own business and do their own thing, regardless of the compelling need.

Finally, someone else, a Samaritan, approaches the dying man; and, unlike the ones who preceded him, he responds in a very different manner. Although he is of a different race, a different religion and a different culture than the injured man, he takes the necessary action. Lovingly, he tends to the man's wounds, pouring in oil and wine. He

The Samaritan's philosophy—What's Mine is Yours—permeated his actions and his attitudes.

then loads the man on his own donkey for the arduous 10-mile journey into the city. Upon arriving there, he pays for the wounded man's lodging and care, even promising the innkeeper to pay more, if necessary.

PRACTICING THE PRINCIPLES

The Samaritan's philosophy—*What's Mine is Yours*—permeates his actions and his attitudes. His behavior sets an example we are to follow today as we live out the Principle of Sacrificial Giving in our stewardship. Our challenge is to look at our lives and ask honestly, what would God have me give sacrificially for His sake? There are people in desperate need today—physically, emotionally, and spiritually desperate—and God uses other people to meet such needs. As the Samaritan's actions saved a man's life, we too can be instruments used of God in His miraculous work of redemption. As true believers it is imperative that we look at all of our resources and say resoundingly, *Lord, What's Mine is Yours!* This must be our philosophy, for without this spirit of sacrifice we cannot and will not mature and succeed spiritually.

When your church has a major need, give sacrificially to meet it. As a member of the body, your participation is crucial, especially at times of special need. Whether it is for a new building, a debt retirement project or some other kind of ministry expansion, your sacrificial involvement will be a blessing both personally and corporately.

When your neighbor has a major problem, give sacrificially to solve it. Be a Samaritan, and be open to what is going on in the lives around you. Be sensitive to what's happening with them and be responsive in the ways that you are able. It may demand the sacrifice of time more than money, of emotional energy more than financial assistance; but whatever it takes, be an instrument of Christ's love.

When your Christian brother or sister has a major crisis, give sacrificially to confront it. Think, for example, about believers who are being persecuted for their faith, many of them punished for the "crime" of serving Jesus. Their sacrifice is an inspiration to us, and it should also motivate us to sacrifice, too, with "Good Samaritan" gifts on their behalf.

Only you know the meaning of "sacrifice" in your life. Whatever it is, pray earnestly that God would enable you to serve Him and give to Him in a truly sacrificial manner.

Scripture References:
[1] Mark 12:43-44
[2] Luke 10:25-29
[3] Luke 10:30-37

15

WHO'S ON YOUR TEAM?

*Oneness of heart and mind
brings greatness of power and witness.*

You probably don't know who Theodore Maiman is, but his scientific developments are an important element of your daily life. Dr. Maiman perfected the first commercially viable laser. His breakthrough device was a small rod made of ruby crystals which was set inside a cylinder. At either end of the cylinder is affixed a mirror, one end fully reflective and the other only partially silvered so that a strong light can pass through. Through a flash tube coiled around the cylinder, flashes of light are fired into the rod. The atoms along the rod then become "excited" and pro-

The first Christians were united in their attitude toward material possessions, and in their witness to Christ's resurrection—and in that unity was power.

duce tiny bursts of light called photons. These photons collide with the atoms, exciting them to produce more and more photons until the tube is filled with them bouncing back and forth from mirror to mirror. The amount of photons becomes so great that they pass right through the partially reflective mirror. This remarkable effect is the laser beam.

A medium-powered laser and a medium-wattage light bulb can actually have the same number of photons. However, the light bulb has the strength only to warm one's hand while the laser can cut through steel. Why such a huge difference? In the light bulb, the photons keep bouncing around randomly. In the laser, they line up, unifying to produce phenomenal power. The difference lies in the strength of unity.

In the spiritual realm, unity produces great power as well. When believers unify, the result is potent. Take the example of the Christians on the Day of Pentecost, shortly after Jesus had ascended to heaven. The Book of Acts tells us that "All the believers were one in heart and mind. No one claimed that any of his possessions was his own, but they shared everything they had. With great power the apostles continued to testify to the resurrection of the Lord Jesus, and much grace was upon them all."[1] They were unified in heart and mind. They were unified in their attitude toward material possessions. They were unified in testifying to Christ's resurrection truth. And in their unity they experienced "great power."

When believers unite to give, as those first Christians gave, an undeniable power results. This is a key precept of stewardship, the Principle of Unified Giving. It's the law which teaches us that *oneness of heart and mind brings greatness of power and witness.* When an offering must be taken, for example, the more unified the participants, the more powerful the impact. God's design and His desire is that we work in spiritual partnership, not as sole proprietors. "Lone rangers" cannot experience the exhilarating joy of spiritual unity.

Earlier in the same chapter of Acts, we read of the bold ministry of Peter and John and the price they paid for proclaiming the message of Jesus. Because they would not keep quiet about their Lord...because they were convinced that their silence would carry eternal consequences...because their faith was in the One whose Name is above all others...they didn't give up or give in. Although the authorities demanded that they cease to teach about Jesus or even to speak His name, they refused and were put in prison. They remained united in their determination and commitment, and it had the effect of a spiritual laser cutting straight through the heart of a godless culture.[2]

When Peter and John were released from jail, they returned to their fellow Christians and joined them in prayer and fellowship. All the believers recog-

nized the risks they were taking, but in the larger context,
the threats didn't matter.
Consequently, their prayers
were not filled with expressions of anxiety; instead, they
overflowed with the promises
of Scripture. Their emotions

God's design and His desire is that we work in spiritual partner-ship, not as sole proprietors.

and thoughts were anchored in the reality of who God
is. No one pretended that the circumstances were
pleasant, but everyone confessed two essential
truths—that God is sovereign and that He is forever
the Creator. They were absolutely, resolutely unified
in these truths.

The same God to whom those first century
disciples devoted their lives, that same Sovereign Lord
and Creator, is our God. And when we serve Him in
unity we are actively confiding in the One who is
greater than the one who dominates this world's system. In response to our faithful service, He can create
new dispositions in the hearts of our opponents. He

can create a thirst for Jesus in the hearts of those who once rejected the Gospel. He can create new circumstances to override the prevailing circumstances. And He can do all this because He is greater than all.

PRACTICING THE PRINCIPLES

Practically speaking, how can we live by the Principle of Unified Giving? Here are three effective ways:

Think of fellow Christians as your partners. To perceive others as partners is to perceive yourself as a partner, and that's a good thing spiritually. Paul was thankful to other Christians for their "partnership in the Gospel"[3] as they united with him in prayer, in work and in financial support. Partnership has numerous beneficial effects and enables us to experience the power of unity.

Think of your gifts to the Lord's work as contributions to a unique mutual fund. In the financial realm, mutual funds incorporate the contributions of thousands of individuals who have pooled their monies to share in the benefits of something very large. In the spiritual realm, all that we give for the Lord's sake is an investment in "God's mutual fund", and it pays dividends beyond imagination.

Think of your church as a laser, not a light bulb. When a congregation is truly united in service and stewardship, the impact is powerful. It's like a steel-cutting laser versus a dim-watted light bulb. Unity in spirit and purpose turns a body of believers into a force for righteousness.

Scripture References:
[1] Acts 4:32-33
[2] Acts 4:1-31
[3] Philippians 1:5

16

—GIVING ZEALOUSLY—
ARE YOU POSITIVELY CONTAGIOUS?

*Zealous stewardship spreads
like a powerful contagion.*

His name was Simon, but we know him better by the descriptor that follows his name: the Zealot. Unlike his famous namesake, Simon Peter, who became the most prominent of the Twelve Apostles, Simon the Zealot is virtually unknown to us. Not a single word he ever said or a single deed he ever did is recorded in the Scriptures. The only thing the Bible tells us about Simon is that he was a Zealot. Yet, in this one potent word we can see a man of flaming enthusiasm. Like the peephole in a wooden fence through which one can view a vast landscape, this

When Simon put his faith in Jesus and accepted Him as Messiah, he abandoned his old commitment and embraced a completely new one.

word "Zealot" reveals a great deal to us.

In Jesus' day, the Zealots were a loosely-structured group of what we would today call guerrilla fighters. They were fiercely committed to liberating Palestine from Roman tyranny, and those who joined with the Zealots had to go through a "conversion" experience, selling themselves out to the cause. As a Zealot, Simon had to be a certain kind of person. He had to be an idealist, thinking his side could actually win. He had to be a visionary, looking ahead to the liberation of his people. He had to be sincere, believing the cause to be right. And he had to be dedicated, so dedicated that he would willingly give his life in the struggle.

When Simon put his faith in Jesus and accepted Him as Messiah, he abandoned his old commitment and embraced a completely new one. He had found something more important than the cause; indeed, he had found the One whom the Jewish people had for centuries longed for: the Christ. He had met the true Liberator, and nothing would ever be the same. Simon did not cease to be the impassioned person he was before; rather, he discovered a new focus for that zealousness and passion. From that point forward, his life was dedicated to service and stewardship as a disciple of Jesus Christ. According to first century historians, Simon ultimately gave his life for Christ, dying as a martyr for his Lord.

Simon personified the Principle of Zealous Giving which is described by Paul in the first verses of 2 Corinthians 9: "There is no need for me to write to you about this service to the saints," he begins, "for I know your eagerness to help, and I have been boasting about it to the Macedonians, telling them that since last year you in Achaia were ready to give; and your enthusiasm has stirred most of them to action."[1]

Godly zeal is a powerful force which has a positively contagious effect on other believers. When the Corinthian Christians gave eagerly and enthusiastically it motivated the Macedonians to do likewise.

To be zealously ready as a servant and steward of Jesus Christ is to live with a heightened sense of responsiveness to God's leading. It is not to be fanatical but to be radical, for true Christianity *is* radical because it is a life lived in radical opposition to all the forces of the world, the flesh and the devil. True Christianity belongs neither to the left nor to the right in the political realm. True Christianity is neither conservative nor liberal in the social realm. True Christianity is not of this earth but of heaven. It is not temporal but eternal. It is not bound by the natural, but is lived within the supernatural boundaries of God's grace. True Christianity belongs to another level, another dimension. It is life on a different plane.

Sometimes Christians become fanatical, going off on tangents or giving their time and energies to causes rather than to Christ. Such fanatical behavior is usually prompted either by a misunderstanding of God's Word, misapplication of God's truth or sin in some area of life that has created the need for a spiritual smokescreen. But the zealous giver is motivated by the pure desire to use every resource to please God and fulfill His purposes.

The driving purpose of fanaticism is the cause or activity itself. The purpose of Christian zeal, however, is a Person, Jesus Christ Himself.

The Principle of Zealous Giving confirms that enthusiasm is a good thing if it is directed toward a godly purpose. The purpose of fanaticism is the cause or activity or idea itself. The purpose of Christian zeal, however, is a Person, Christ Himself. "I am the gate,"[2] Jesus said categorically. The essence of Christianity is not a cause, a philosophy, a religion or an idea. It is a Person. Who He is, what He has done, why He is. These are the things that truly matter.

PRACTICING THE PRINCIPLES

In the context of biblical stewardship, zealousness is a Christ-centered passion to give everything for His sake. It is all-encompassing, enfolding all that one is capable of giving: money, time, influence, help, counsel or a thousand-and-one other things. The motive behind the giving is the indwelling love of Christ. "For Christ's love compels us,"[3] Paul explained in his second letter to the Corinthians. Whereas the religious fanatics of today's world are motivated by anger, guilt or fear, the believer is compelled by love. Having been set free from the penalty of sin we are now enabled to live in triumph over the power of sin. In this regard, the zealous Christian experiences a victory that is profoundly spiritual.

See only Christ as the Cause. When Simon joined the Zealots he probably had no reservations. Most likely, he gave himself wholly to the cause. But then he learned of the One greater than any cause, the Lord Jesus Christ. Still a zealous man, Simon redirected his zeal to serve the only one worth serving. His instructions came directly from the Lord, who taught him what it meant to be a disciple. He heard it when Jesus said, "If anyone would come after me, he must deny himself and take up his cross and follow me."[4] He was there when Jesus said, "Any of you who does not give up everything he has cannot be my disciple."[5] And he was listening when the Lord said, "I tell you the truth, no one who has left home or brothers or sisters or mother or father or children or fields for me and the gospel will fail to receive a hundred times as much in this present age...and in the age to come, eternal life."[6] Simon was listening, and he took the words to heart; as indeed we should, too.

Count only Christ as dear. As we put into practice the principles of Christ-centered stewardship there is an ever-growing realization that these are principles of discipleship as well, for stewardship is inextricably linked to discipleship. To be a disciple is to be a steward; to be a steward is to be a disciple. In both respects (as disciples and as stewards), our priority is not ourselves but the Lord. Forsaking everything else, we count only Christ as dear. With zealous readiness, we say with Paul, "I consider my life worth nothing to me, if only I may finish the race and complete the task the Lord Jesus has given me—the task of testifying to the gospel of God's grace."[7]

Scripture References:
[1] 2 Corinthians 9:1-2
[2] John 10:9
[3] 2 Corinthians 5:14
[4] Mark 8:34
[5] Luke 14: 33
[6] Mark 10:29-30
[7] Acts 20:24